WOOD

LAND

WOODLAND

poetry, prose and illustrations
by
caroline holm

To my feral Jane Eden who holds my heart.
May you always taste your wildness.

Paperback: 978-1-7378550-3-3
Hardcover: 978-1-7378550-2-6
Blurb Paperback: 978-1-7378550-1-9
Blurb Hardcover: 978-1-7378550-0-2

Edited by Kristin Berger
Cover art by Caroline Holm
Layout by Caroline Holm
Book art by Caroline Holm
Author photo by Daishja Brown

Untethered Press
Salem, Oregon
www.carolineholmpoetry.com

Printed in the United States of America.

"What does it mean that the earth is so beautiful?
What shall I do about it?"

-Mary Oliver

CONTENTS

AUTUMN EQUINOX & MIDWINTER

Little Roots

It is no surprise that our hands would look like little roots.
What are we doing with our sense of touch
if not connecting and expanding
and if each time we grasp, we plant
what should we hold onto?

Our fingers and toes would stretch right down into the gloried soil
if we only loved the earth well enough
and we might become deeply embedded into one another
if we simply learn to draw near.

That lovers would share a heart only makes sense—
bone grows to bone and flesh to flesh
when one touches anything long enough.

Animals

Animals do not need
to strive or struggle
to tend the earth
as we do.

Their simple being is a song of soft praise
their rising and sleeping, an effortless rhythm
their gathering and their hunting
a drumming beat, a thud of vitality
a thanksgiving to the dense forest.

Their roaming, their nurturing, their birthing
and even their death
leave their loving soil richer
and more melodious
than what came before them.

Order

Do you suppose the mighty black bear
ever thinks his own body too much
or that wilted petals turned dust
regret their having fallen?
Nature does her calling and the order of all follows suit.

I don't think the summer plants mute
when they stop their striving and fall over
or curse the woolly-headed clover
for taking over my yard
and I don't scold the salamander's scar
from maybe a frightful journey.

We all take part in a melodic turning
and the earth is at peace with her stages
marked by impermanence in pages
but a less solemn song could not come
for even death has its drum
in this place of symphony.

Delivering Woods

I want so badly to plant my fingers
plumb center in the Maker's soil
and grow a whole new self.
I want my nail beds to take root
and bloom right there in nature's wealth
I want to be naked
to be honest and green
to don the frock of the earth
the licorice fern's earnest sheen
to be wind-strewn into all submission,
to scale the saplings with winged permission
to be brothers with the rows of crows
and sisters with the flurried leaves
and taking after them, my friends
to ever shed and ever mend
and to fall, to fall, to fall
into all of everything.

Nature of You

Your body holds a nature that mirrors the earth's own charm:
wrapping veins present as sprawling vines
ivy climbs the arc of eyebrow
sweltering dew drips from stem neck to garnet thigh
the quartz gleam of animal teeth
shores for skin—
the very sheath of you.

Inside a home of moth spirit, sacred soil, oak will
bloody roots and muddy organs weave for us our place
in this tangled creaturehood.

Bare feet planted in dirt, our taproots grounded
and fingers as insects busy with their work
tying twine of hesitance
burrowing through the given earth
for remains of forlorn hearts and sense
of meaning and of worth.

Lichen freckles spot the thorny villages of you
and forehead creases are subdued
by the old moss of your thoughts
feathered melodies fall from you as you sing
your bough arms sway and swing
and almost everything on this earth calls back to you
if you're listening.

Autumnal

Growing fairer and fairer until
God's own art thy only will.
Thy gold displayed without an ill
and reddest hues from windowsill

and though your morning is colder still
and your night grows ever dark
it is here I behold
the fire sent by heaven's spark.

Time steals all from you, it's true
and, yes, your glory fades
but what bright light does not retire
and what sun won't rise another day?

There is much time for berries' heat
and even more still for the spring
and winter always has her say
in the order of everything

but autumn's day now is here
and her call draws so nigh
that it would be such tragedy
to miss her scarlet sigh

to miss the shivering fever
sent by auburn fields all burned
to know her grace and then to leave her
from such beauty to ever turn.

For now, I rest in fallen leaves
in the meadows all gone dim.
The flowers here have faded
but we may still taste their whim.

This, our lesson on attachment
for what has been abandoned more
than the trees that shed their every garment
upon the forest floor?

Fungi

Whispers of the fruiting forest
scarlet, supple, sand
tangible magic
light breath in hand.

We take them in
their touch, their stand
their stem, their glow, that stretching fan.
Their gills so porous, a creature skin
and spores, their stores of wonderment.

Mycelium take flight down underfoot
and until now we've looked to what may be seen
but, darling, whole worlds dwell beneath our feet.

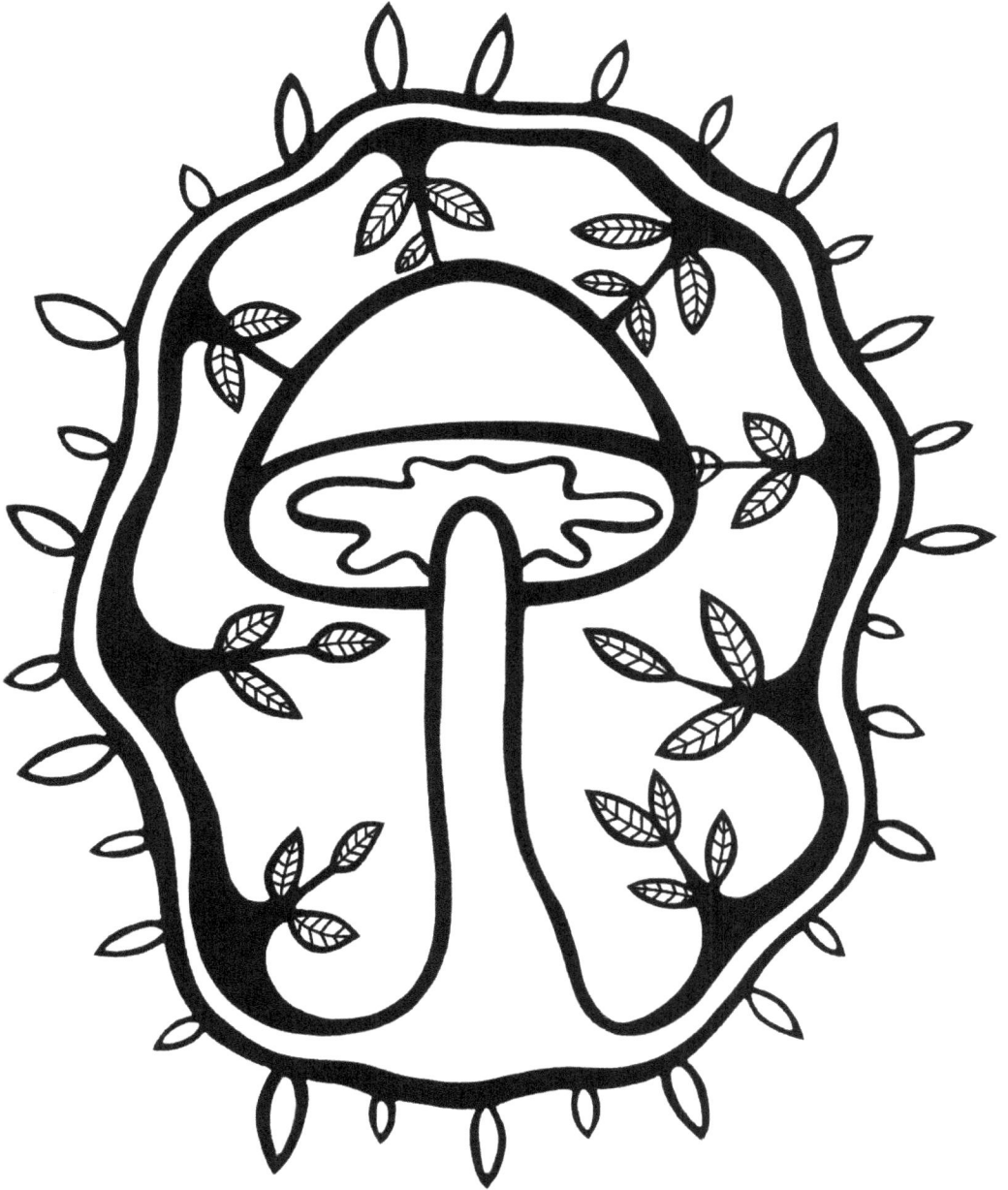

Cleansing

Fickle friend you are but still we sing
September hymns of autumn's wing
the miracle of that frightful thing
that sweeps from us what summer brings

and scarlet leaves cry like silver bells
and wake the wishing from its wells
much too soon for us to tell
if this is magic or discarded spell.

The sky pours forth clouded hope to thee
and by winter nights, we might still see
earth's wayward beauties, those sweeping scenes
that ask the heart, unbruise; ask the welt, unsting.

This is autumn calling
everything at once now falling—
the earth inviting you to rest.

The healing is here in the icy blue
in slumbering depths, in sauntering through;
in the long-blurred dawn, in trees shedding new
in the pain, in the ache, in the cold, cleansing dew
and our skin now seeping with only that which rings true.

Common Grace

With leaves burned scarlet on the tips
I swore I'd burn my hand to bits
still I reached to grasp, could not resist
and instead was met with autumn's kiss

and the ashen gray that we've cursed to know
holds within a way to grow.
Seeds still flourish here below
with virtue painted pure as snow.

The air we expect to cruelly freeze
our soft skin, our knobby knees
does more for us than we believe—
even winter stings hold decency.

A common grace is set in place
that we bathe in and dare to gaze:
the ways of skin on other skin
the ideas we catch, the breath within
the age-old power of oak persistent
the way its roots take back what man has hidden.

It's the peat carpet growing upon forest floor
granted even to those who do not adore.
The return of golden summer
when we lay and beg for more.

It's the chapel made here by conifer beams
arch of branch ceiling and the praying breeze
every bloom bowing to winter decrees
and sermons caught wind of from elder bees.

It's the birth and then the death
the sacred life and sacred breath
that whirl around this earth, wind-swept
filling air with metaphor and meaning in every step.

To even the neglectful who have fallen from view
who have poisoned the plants
who have tried to subdue
space to roam this gloried-earth is due
a stone to sit, a sky to view

and beyond this earthen shadow or type
lies soil more true, more pure, more ripe
crying out through earth's every nuanced hue
to the heart of me, to the heart of you.

Photograph

Daisy fields, a tender kiss on pink eyelids
leaning on ancient oak with you
in patches of the only winter warmth
we'd known all year

wondering if those kids were really headed
to dive in the February river
if that amber-bellied robin
really did sing more softly than the rest.

My wrist still bares the scar—
token of a thorny bracelet
and I still wear your gossamer sentences
as my finest dress.

Lichen and Seeds

I brought you promises empty
hands filled with lichen and seeds.
came baring my roles without mending
and fell barreling through thorny weeds.

I learned through all of my lack
what nutrients one needs to grow
a harvest worth the labor
a bloom even through snow.

Bitter Drink

Maybe the ache is better
than the having and the holding
and the questions far weightier
than the answers and the knowing.

Maybe your words could ring
without your making a sound
and shadows might finally sing
if we'd let them abound.

Maybe my lines are halved
and maybe they are whole.
Maybe the heart is empty
but what if it is full?

Maybe it all reaches much deeper
than mycelium, roots and core
and the soil is calling out to us
through death for more.

I'm not sure if the hour has passed
or if it ever came
but I know, at once, at last
there is no single soul to blame

for this wisdom cannot stack
and the meaning of these words won't sink
if we won't taste the honeyed lack
if we won't sip the bitter drink.

Slumbering

Even beauty may reach a point
of peaking til it burns
and those who fly too high won't know
how to still beneath the ferns.

Staying low, a loveliness—
kneeling may be best.
Doing may seem like bravery
but courage mounts in rest.

Twofold

Is there much to be said
about the sharp but fond knife of morning air
or the nearly absurd optimism of the rusted robin
when the sun first returns from his deep slumber?
If there is, I will say it.

Is there much to be done
about the cracked front porch step
the trees have had their way with
or the forgiveness of the warmed pavement
on naked, craving feet
thawing stiff bones—easy and sweet
or the way winter hides our dearest star
in its swallowing velvet white?
If there is, I will do it.

Is there much to be made
of words trapped on your tongue
hanging in their immaculate and striking silence
only making their escape by finally pouring
from the corners of your pursed lips
as wanted milk from a shattered pitcher
or your arms crossed over your chest tight as iron gates
locked with their reasoning, protecting the tree
two folds I want only to climb into?
If there is, I will make it.

Snow

Like snow, like gold. how things unfold
how your purity leaves me blind

like brick-thick night, all dazed, white light
and dead bronze dust on emerald ferns bright

like bushes of tart berries in a famine,
milk and honey, a sun-soaked promised land
and quartz found in the barren sand

like the unfurling of an unmappable plan
or the tender weight of a copper-freckled hand—

you are everything that is right.

Siren Seasons

Around and around counting all as found
though the prying wind never seems to learn
from her ways and waltzes with
the gold-dipped July fern

and the siren rain fell
as autumn's spell on all the hearts of men.
Down too I went and still was sent
to rise right up again.

On and on a lenient dawn
flutters a singed October leaf
and the sun, as he does, is darting in and out
of a graying, grizzly grief.

For what he mourns, I do not know
but still would count a treason
to curse the moods we find him in
to curse the waves of season.

Each month will spill from windowsills
from rain gutters and reason
each day will play the notes it's meant
each week will shed its meaning.

Each morning pours from skies in scores
and every navy night grows younger
tying down the moon, the creatures that swoon
as it fills the swirling under.

I no longer resist December deaths
or January thunder
I need only to pause and slow the breath
to see it all as wonder

for time is not a place we're caught
not a prison or a stage
but the giving, living impermanence—
that blessed passing from page to page.

PRIMAVERAL

Birdsong

It started with a single airy chirp that clumsily fell out as if from the mouth of an infant—gentle and imperfect but terribly certain. Then his peers joined in with their far more frantic calls. The elders also took off thinking that they might show them which edges to soften, that they ought to lead in their own clever way. A handful of breeds joined in total, all clashing, all colliding, and they all had their say. I couldn't tell where they came from nor make out where one trill ended and another began. Their notes thickened and formed layers so muddied, so ruddied that, stacked on top of one another, their chorus rang out like a siren.

I suppose I could attempt to define each call. I could try to peel apart the sheets and make some sense and symbol of each sound in singularity. But who could ever separate such immaculate chaos?

Eventually, it got so heavy that I could no longer hear the stray dog in the far off field or make out the train from over the bridge passing by the riverfront. I didn't hear the crow crying around the corner and I couldn't hear my own thoughts if I had tried. Their calls piled up so high that they even challenged the trees. Their keys hung thicker on the bark than its own native moss and soon even the air was consumed until it was no longer my breath that was released by my sighs but their mad melodies. I had come to know them as rightly as I knew my own skin and my own blood, companions to my very being. But I learned that even constancy is not constant.

As the sun calmed, so did they. Without warning and without yielding, the flurry halted. They retreated and turned their hymns back into branches, pulled their echoes back into the roots and tucked their volumes away between the rings of the trees. Once again, the dog bark struck me, the train pressed on, the crow kept at his crying and all of my old thoughts returned. Before long, it was as if it hadn't happened at all. The waters that it parted sealed back up and all of the earth around me appeared unaltered.

There was, however, one thing changed by it. It had embedded itself into my very body. Their call became my mindless hum, my sympathetic soundtrack and my solace—so much so that at night, as I shut my eyes to enter into the boundless world, it is their harp that I hear and it is their song that I sing.

Spring Greed

We opened our greedy mouths to benevolent cherry blossoms
on those, the first days of fragile spring
when the lingering rain still teased
the bitter air would still freeze
but the enduring plants pressed on

and every maddening dawn
grew even more arresting
as we lay and watch the thrushes
so devout in their nesting—
their music more charity than chore.

Daily the sun swept the night
and even the rain joined the fight
to knock us down on awe-struck knees
among the fern and the fauna, their feral delight
and the sage, succoring bees.

Each morning we licked wild daffodils
and the grasses they'd adorned
fervently lapped up pine pollen from the foliage floor
pressed open every ivy door
and not once did we relent
in our heaven days all spent
in our fevered search
for more and more.

Feral Eden

There's been a halo over her since the day she was born
and all of her springtime wisdom subdued our winter scorn.
With crimson cherub grin, rose lips and white fire hair
she laid our debts to rest and left hearts impossibly bare.

There is no silence I would not fill
with her voice, with her thoughts
no space I would not be caught
by the untamable image of her.

Eyes of light, all within sight
and truly, to her, for the taking.
I hope only that she does more making
than consuming with her days
and I pray that all the rays
of wildness, of wisdom, of wonder
shine her way.

April Guiles

Spring has returned
and I'm ready to trick the red squirrel into thinking that I'm an
animal again
to tell the dogwood tree that I'm just another blossom lying on
his branches
and I am lying on his branches

but is it really such a lie
if I bid my humanness die
and become a part of the pappus for a while
or a bit of that burning breeze
tall grass staining violet knees,
or shriveled petal on stone sidewalk
making the trivial idyllic?

I'm ready to be the fresh growth of the pine needles
that we bite off with such pleasure every April
and I am ready to see what I would not see before
to throw off the old fear of love
and of the wide world
and of the bodily death
as if I were ever only
skin and bone
blood and thought
as if new life didn't follow
every morbid winter.

Filled with Gold

You are all beauty I see:
the moss, the moth, the elderly tree.
Without You, the world is a light switched off
and, to me, a life unlivable
for what is in me that is unforgivable
You have filled with gold
and to every woe you've told
"this life is just the beginning."

so I will keep on living
and smelling Your taffy blossoms
and tasting Your salty seas
and declaring over and over
what a weighty grace You've given me.

Aura

May I touch the light
around your frame
feel your hope and give it a
name
might I know you as different
and one in the same
might I be your sun
may I bring you rain?

Creaturehood

We need not adorn ourselves
with emblems of each passing brand
of contemporary beauty.
Simple creaturehood is enough—

a few common weeds
tangled with the pearl button of the cuff
torn daisies draped over frozen ears
cattail woven through matted hair—
fragments of the imperfectly impermanent,
what nature has left rough.

Scarred, naked feet on opalescent dirt
balmy sweat and worn hands plunged through earth
stained with soil by the garden and with blood by the birth
the kiss of blaring sunrise, cough of campfire hearth
all worlds we may crawl into, each with teachings to be heard.

After all that time alone
weary hearts grow worry prone
but here with you running through prairie fields
with the track marks of blackberry bushes
tracing anklebone patterns
little else matters
but our wildness.

Great Wolf

Great wolf caged, echo of a song so aged
that only the sun sings it now.
May we learn from the daisies just how to bow
and bend to heaven's longing—
forgiving each and every wronging
and bringing our roots to reason.
Make this, at once, the season
that each pest is tended to
and every floral bloom
in the garden you keep
is true.

Honeycomb

I have not loved your hands without flaw
but how your mind has swept me.
We awoke from the dream but still it seems
that your root arms have somehow kept me.

I've not walked with feet like fox—
I've cracked the earth beneath
have crushed the wayward leaf
but your words carry on a long-lost song
with such a grounding relief.

Fingertips likes blackberries weighted with their syrup
course over craving skin
and we form honeycomb sentences
forgiveness forming entrances
with room enough to claim the rough
and space to settle in.

With tempered mouth for cooling off
I do not pretend to scoff
as If I were always dressed in ice white
as If I were never the callous night covering its brightest star
but all of the trail that you are would still lead back to home
for truth and light and comfort roam
all the while knowing that the boundary is you
that the woods are you, that my skin is you
that these words are you.

In the End

Words are wasted weekly—
let these not be just for show.
May my breath be all drawn out
and my sentences now slow.
May the jays do my speaking for me
and the earth, to you, be my touch
while my head is bowed in prayer
and my hands so loosely clutch
the words, the ways, and worries
the dreaded might-have-beens
for what could be is part of everything
and nothing
in the end.

The Garden We Keep

At night, the words you bring
come bottled, an ocean offering
I take them in, devour them
and send my own to servant sea.

I've set at last my heart on casts
more sturdy than the oak.
I count on you, your burgeoning true
and wear your worn-down olive coat.

No less unfeigned are these blooms now
than when you gave to me
your night sky gaze, your mending ways
and regard on bended knee.

I rest in this—a wounded kiss
a warm mercy now unfolding.
Lifted hand, this skin and man
our wounds, our hopes emboldening.

The garden we keep
sowed here in sheets deep,
in words and promises kept
in the tie between eyes,
nectar compromise
in shared, in bared fears and flesh.

For Life's Sake

I am but an animal
here for all to see
and I promise that you won't see much
when you take a look at me.

I am but an animal
naked body, wild earth
I've clawed here for centuries
marked red by all the birth.

I am but an animal
extension of the whole
and every living thing you meet
lives within my soul.

I am but an animal
and clover honey caught my step
but I've paced since then have sharpened
and have learned to tame the breath.

I am but an animal
here with my musings to make
about mating and the madness
of life for life's own sake.

Heaven Thought

Tell not oft a heaven thought
unless it should lift some soul.
Spread not here a narrow tongue
lest it take its leaden toll.

Dart now toward dendritic purpose
free the shadows, run with fire
free the feral heart's good fury
and air out perfumed desire.

The words and burdens are nearly lifted
and the present days grow so small.
Loosely hold the riches gifted
knowing that all things do fall.

When others praise you by an image
or title of fine expectancy
then shed the skin, the weight, the privilege
and set your servant heart to sea

for to be claimed and to be carried
surely, these a wonder
but to this life and body be married
is to know the scorn of thunder.

Begin

What really am I
what really are you
what of the ephemeral we once held in view?
What is purely physical, solely sacred too
and what would come to be if all were taken from you?

What really lies within
and what ever lies without?
What lies of id pour madly
pour gladly from our mouths?

What airy pollen or licking dew
won't fade by morning
won't flee from you?
What skin, what mind
won't stretch, won't shrink
doesn't decline and won't cease to think?

What absolving rain or ocean cry
could we claim as ours, might we lie beside?
What will last, won't turn to ash
and what will depart again?
What heart, once full, does not soon empty
and what earthly love does not descend?

There is fullness. I know it as nourishment now
more than temporal, more than skin—
a spirit, a Way, a breath within.

Beyond all time and the concocted now
a river runs freely with all it endows
and if you're still counting that singing wren
merely two-dimensional—what folly, friend.
These forms contain more than feeling and seeing
a layer of life not dependent on men
where we are all as one
and, as such, let us begin.

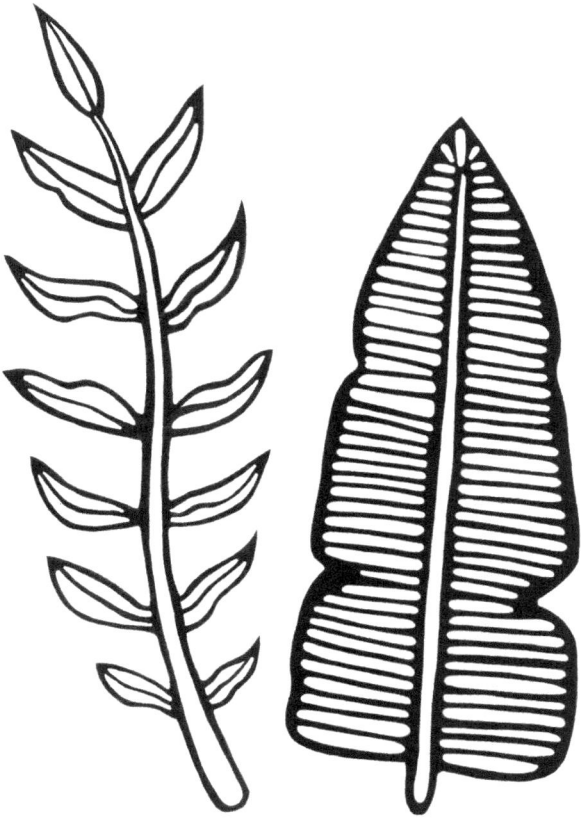

Nature Takes Back

Nature takes back and does so with such grace
no matter the poisons or ways we replace
her beauty and valor with what calculates
or try to destroy the backdrop of fates.

The earth cries and roars as she weeps at torn views
she lives and she dies, she feels and subdues.
No less the present, the alive or the true
no less the immovable stubbornness of you.

She does not go softly but quakes with destruction
when the veins of amoral industry shake with corruption
and we heed, how we need her ancient instruction
when we're blinded by convenience and industry's abduction.

Fences of government, monocrops we abuse—
she too has her sentence, her thorny dues.
How you sit and declare from the shallowest pews
without tasting the nectar or naming the hues.

You will see emerald ivy overtaking iron vine
retrieving what's been stolen and forced in line.
She will not be stamped out by cities or towers
for she too has her signals, her energy, her hour.

SUMMERTIDE

Amber Honey

I want new blossoms
and amber honey so heavy on my tongue
that I, for once, cannot speak
pollen falling from my eyelashes,
weighing them down to rest for weeks
with every bat and every blink.
I want more elderberry wine to drink
than I know what to do with.
I want far more firelight in my days
and I want your gaze, your gaze, your gaze.

I want lavender linens to bathe my skin
dresses of crepe paper moss so thin
to float while I go around and around.
I want the hymns of ancient winds
and every vine to tangle in
and I want you near, I want you near, I want you near.

I want the ground, the dirt, the roots
between my fingertips and toes
to feel the warming pulse of
I want flower petals caught
in the lacings of my worn boots
that mean that I lie down in roses
and I rise with sunshine.
I want a softer touch
yet to hold just as much as I'm meant to
and I want you, I want you, I want you.

Good-Natured

We cannot in this machine of life
with all of its madness and all of its sadness
know at every turning corner what to say
or where next to plant our uncertain feet.

What we can do is lie down still for a moment
near the good-natured meadow
in the deep and scalded summer grass that swallows us up
that strokes our sun-singed cheeks
while it threatens to grow over us a while.

Follow me down
where the Mormon crickets whisper
where the obliging stream plays her foaming keys
and we'll wait for what the ceilings of trees have to teach us.

Ants

Black ants have taken to my sunspot
here in the best corner of the lawn
deep in the fractal green
beneath my big samara tree
that I have memorized the movement of.

I suspect that they too know the goodness
of being warmed to the core
of wearing the sun's glory as your own
the goodness of lying down, utterly still, half a foot deep
in the thick wildflowers and stocky weeds
until you've forgotten the body you came here in.

Soil

I stand, at last
on a firm foot planted
life well-enchanted
after seasons of illness and sorrow
my pockets filled with all that I've borrowed:
the sundry mercies of men
the wily wisdoms and then
the still, silent words of the forest.

For once, in heart, the poorest
now granted such true joy
and what else could I employ but awe?
When the body crumbled, the spirit called
and all that had weakened, strengthened
all that had shortened, lengthened
and how the soul pressed on.

What else could I pay but humble thanks
when held bare on druzy river banks.
On the ground, in the dirt, it's here that I'll sing
of how the earth to us is a maternal thing
when mothering is just what we need.

What does soil hold within
but evidence of earth as kin—
ancestors rooted in love and mourning?
What is birth but light ringing rife
and death but an offering
in this brief and breaking breath of life?

When I Return

When I return home
if my book is not coated in moss
if my hands and feet are not muddied
if my hair is not tangled with Queen Anne's lace and twigs
if I'm not walking upside down and sideways
with mad and wild wonder for the world in which we live—
send me back out again.

I have more to learn
more shutting up to do
more stillness to seek.

Growing

If my skin were to grow
might it grow with a daisy grace
and could it feed the heart's own glowing
with each wrinkled praise?

And if my skin were to expand
might it stretch into fierce sea
and be washed by waves of redemption
if they did not swallow me?

If my skin was swelling
and this heart was gathered too
might they flow with unashamed legacy
might they live on in love with you?

What if my skin was growing
but instead of shrinking down
I loved this soul's old shell so well
that I deemed it tender crown?

If this skin did extend
and I did not drag my feet
I could plant my very toes
in the forgiving earth beneath.

If this skin is growing
I will not buckle knees
but leap with the glory weight of it
and kiss it into pastured peace.

If this skin is growing
perhaps the weight of the world will shrink
and leave room enough to claim the rough
and, on tangible eternity, to think and think.

Strands

My strands of hair are roots that weave
deep into soil and thread through trees
tangle in flower beds with laboring bees
and splay as flaxen hay where lilac moths now sleep

golden ropes to throw to weeds
to pull them up upon their knees
to sweep their way in kindly breeze
to stroke the clovers, to thank and please

locks that braid in with the leeks
that stretch down rivers and bathe in creeks
that, all too often, aim to seek
something more than the common or meek
as they stretch right up to heaven's peak.

Sunbathing

Come out from the shade and be remade
as the skies reborn each morning.
Stretched out on the lawn, bathed in birdsong
curling burnt limbs now toward perfection.

Even the grasses' good reflection could not tell you otherwise
for here you are as alive as the potent rose
the fervent hornet, the mighty thorn.

We are all worn down to the very bone by stony industry
and it takes little but a moment of rest as earthen guest
to see fallible skin, sun-kissed, as blessed.

Ivy

Time spreads out like thick ivy
and I, as so many, do not see
the growth and shoots of every root
for all of its fragility.

Time spreads out like pure minerals
across a salty blue sea
as it coats each creature with a pinch of kindness
and each with a bit of cruelty.

Time spreads out like serried clovers
all spread in bed upon my lawn.
On my idle May days
I may wish them away
but, one by one, they return
by dawn.

Time spreads out like your tonic hands
coursing over my seashore back
tracking and tracing
as new wave, new land
but retreating
now leaving
too fast.

Reverie

I don't think that I've said the finest words
or that my sentences will ever settle.
I know only that if I don't write, I turn to dust
and that the things I'm seeing deserve the simple trust
of being made permanent somewhere:

catching the pollen in the lacey air
getting a face full of shell roses
and taking the biggest breath one can
an easy place on earth to stand
or coupled river stones to slip from
the brush rabbit's far off thumping drum
and the birch moss slyly growing

the way learning that not knowing
is never a bad thing
if our eyes, our ears and our hearts
remain wide open.

Magnolias

I am trying to be as the magnolia now
and bloom more softly this season
to be just as the seeds that heed
and persist with little reason.

Warm Cedar

Warm cedar eyes and no compromise
and a will as sure as steel.
Here you stand, fierce temperament in hand
and tongue ever in cheek.
You, the ephemeral garden
you, the grappling peak
and is anything true ever easy?

Beneath a lapis lazuli sky where the lone crickets cry
the weight of your chest is heaving heaven's breath.
We take two leaps but reach one depth.

Copper pollen spots as if from the bees
that trot, that plot, that paint the knees,
the very honey of you.
No less will ever do
than to lie still on rough river banks
singing earth-praise and giving thanks
with the body, the mind and the spirit of you.

Your Rhythm

You are an ever-waking bloom
in spite of every noon
I have ever come to meet.
You are the saccharine slowness
and then the lifting peak
the blue I drown in, the one as deep
as water below, the to and fro
of oneness and sound that ever resound-
I've listened to your rhythm forever.

You do well suit a lily or a rose
quartz and minerals of untamed beauty
even the gray, you complement.
Yes, you suit me well too.
As garments, I put you on and I do not take you off
I wear your loveliness as my loveliness
a thief of your magic-
I listen to your rhythm forever.

You are a warning sign, the turning of a mind
and the wading in waters that liberate.
I covet your time, your wisdom that binds.
As the granting of pleas, rest for worn knees
is your hand on my face-
I'll listen to your rhythm forever.

Hallelujahs

How many times have I opened a gaping mouth
to offerings of sticky berries
ripe with healing and skin revealing
goodness, vitality and wild strife?

How often in this fleeting life
have I been gifted the summer air
sweet and heavy on the tongue, pooling sugar in the lungs
hanging heavy here in August's citrine sun?

What, again, was it that I ever thought I needed?
I've forgotten it now in this world of Eden
and for what more could I ever ask
when it was an honor to brush the blade of grass?

It is all, it is all, it is all too much
to witness the world, to feel your touch.

Harvesting Hour

Let us live and breathe and love and kiss
with an air of urgency.
Let us learn to think, to praise and resist
on our winding paths to free.

All masks do crack, all roses wilt
all gloom, all doom decays
the summer sun flees from us
the full moon never stays.

There is little time even for me
to move my pen for you.
So many hours that we have neglected to see
and so many thoughts fallen from view.

We must strive to get it right, this fleeting life
or others might get it for us
we must live with awe, so pure and bright
and let the light procure us.

Woodland

Do not take your body for granted
do not let your feet become unplanted
the being is in the grounding
in peace and breath self-surrounding
in cracks and creeks of life so astounding
that they leave me weaving in and out of mere grass blades
with fresh awe.

I envelope myself in little but this:
the earth is a gifted, miraculous wish
of glowing forests that I dreamed of daily from a sickbed
and now weep mirthfully within
light-licked skin, cradled tenderly by instead.

I was daily by dawn's gentle early hand led
to the glow that fell between the leaves
indifferent to days of merriment
and unchanged by those of dread
and it spotted your hand outstretched to me
with flecks of familiar fire
and every light spot seems to me to beckon to aspire
or rest on the flowers simply to please
to stretch on then with remarkable ease
calling virtue into the thoughts of all—
even the hearts of thieves.

By bushes, by mossy branches, by things never planted—
nourished and safe, nurtured and fed
to bask among daisies, to pick the wild herbs
and taste the bitters that the dirt has to offer.

To look just to look and touch only to feel
and know what it is to help a faulting body heal
to know what it is to look at a tree or a babbling brook
and stop, at last, that weightful thinking
that never exhaling and ceaseless unmeaning.

While sitting on a bed of smooth rocks
with worn fingertips and soil-wrestled, petaled locks
being swept up in the most willful forgetting
with a mouth washed by the river
and an animal body bathed in sun—
settling granted by Creator
and a reminder of grace for all I'd done.

Here I did not think of the blood I'd
wretched, of the vials they drew
of legs too frail to lift my body from bed
or of watching my daughter not breathing—
my worries were carried away by sun rays
over a glimmering body stretching on for all days
until I could no longer make them out.
My qualms and queries,
my cowardice thoughts and fear-filled theories
were gone, expelled, finally freed
along with all of my doubt.

It is a great mercy to live to see the rain
bring to us another rich and radiant spring
and a tenderness to be granted the thoughtfulness of the woods
the trees that cover and that hover over every lovely thing—

ceiling of leaves
sheltering thieves as long denied as I.
It is a clemency to have a strong body restored to me
feet to run, hands to tend, eyes to see
this woodland vision's significance and charity.

THE
END.

ACKNOWLEDGMENTS

The making of this book has been impacted by the ripples of more people and experiences than I could ever count. I have always been held by my peers, mentors, family, community and ancestors whether I recognized it or not. My words are not my own but the sum total of everyone who came before me, everyone I've met, every bit of earth and God and miracle I have experienced and everything I have ever seen, heard or read. With the following pages, I'd like to name a few good souls in particular who helped me out a great deal with this book:

Kristin Berger, poet, author and editor of Woodland who encouraged me, went above and beyond in support when I had no idea what I was doing and helped me to turn my dreams into something damn near presentable—thank you. Truly, thank you.

To Alex Ebert whose own work rides the difficult line between profound and playful, who speaks what must be said in this life, who has graciously offered himself as mentor to many artists, whose art has influenced my own for so very long and who somehow caught wind of my words and had encouragement and support to offer that I keep in my pocket for a rainy day— Thank you.

To Eleanor Berry who gave of her time to consider, support and read my work and who generously offered guidance— Thank you.

To Amalie Hill, John Sibley Williams, Kate Gray, Igor Brezhnev and Marc Janssen for considering my work, offering their wisdom and experience and lending me the honor of their encouragement— Thank you.

To the Las Vegas, Portland and Salem poetry communities for providing a space where one can freely create, expand and learn in a safe and welcoming container- Thank you.

To my dear friends Cassia Lopez, Crystal Dutra and Daishja Brown who supported Woodland with their time, their talents and always with their kindness—Thank you.

To my love and closest confidant Joshua Holm who gave of his time, resources and heart to support my art, who believed in and encouraged me to write and make in times when I felt I could not, who inspires me to learn continually and look beyond the physical at each and every moment—Thank you.

To my wild, feral and true Jane Eden who is utterly herself, alive and in awe through it all. This is for and because of you. You are a complicated and miraculous being I will marvel over for the rest of my days and beyond. You awaken my heart and drive me to create. You are the most authentic person I have ever encountered and I have no doubt that you have taught me more than I could ever teach you. My heart finds deep rest when you smile at me. It's an honor to be your mother. I love you so. Thank you.

To all who are fond and familiar, those near and far away, kin and friends and any person who has ever given one breath of their precious life to read half a sentence I've written—Thank you.

To you, dear reader—thank you. May these words meet you in peace and abundance and, when they do not, may they remind you that suffering is the great catalyst of growth and understanding and that belonging is stamped on your very being.

With all of my love and gratitude,
-Caroline

ABOUT THE AUTHOR

Caroline Holm is an Oregon-based visual artist and writer in awe of the natural world and what lies beyond it. She lives and works in the heart of the Willamette Valley where she spends much of her time wandering through local woods with her husband and daughter.

For more of Caroline's work, visit
www.carolineholmpoetry.com
IG: @carolineholmpoetry

www.ingramcontent.com/pod-product-compliance
Lightning Source LLC
Chambersburg PA
CBHW040136270326
41927CB00019B/3404